I Had Forgotten

Verishua Maddix

BookLeaf Publishing

India | USA | UK

Presentation by *BookLeaf Publishing*

Web: www.bookleafpub.com

E-mail: info@bookleafpub.com

ISBN: 9789358318692

First edition 2024

DEDICATION

To my God and my family.

ACKNOWLEDGEMENT

To all my family and friends I love you dearly. Shout out to my mum Iloa, dad Gerald, sister Tenishua. Nieces and nephew Arleigh-Nuura, Nazareth and Exodus. Rochelle who made this possible. And all the glory goes to GOD!!! 🙌🏾

PREFACE

I see this book as an expression of love, fun and rediscovered forgotten memories.

The sky was bewildered grey with flashes of crispy white

The sky was bewildered grey with flashes of
crispy white.
The night was turning into day, or rather the day
was turning into night.
The winter air was bland and cold, unfleeting,
determined and strong.
The townspeople, ice sculptures, pushed along
by the drone of the city.
Soon the sun would come and break their tune,
freeing them up again.
No longer sentinels, ivory, sun-watching, on
droll dulcet days.
But people, flushed, audioed and danced.

The Blood of a Believer

The blood of a believer,
laced with fire.
Infused with purity
and cleansed of worldly desire.

The blood of a believer,
transfused through His pain,
it hums of forgiveness and renews arteries,
vessels and veins.

The blood of a believer,
it sings with new life.
It speaks and it preaches, it declares and it
testifies.

A year in the making

A year in the making, a year in a bowl.
Being stirred up and kneaded and proved,
365 days old.
A year in the making, with my face set to the
son,
A year, I'm still browning, not burnt but not
done.

Teeth

Teeth, good for chewing
Good for biting, don't bite me
Clean with a toothbrush.

Teeth 2

5

Enamel Dentin
Can be made from porcelain
Dentists make money

Utensils

Plastic knives and forks
They snap when I try to eat
Cheap utensils grrr!

The Love of Jesus

The love of Jesus
Can't really write about it,
Not in one Haiku.

The Poet

The Poet said to the Paper, "Let me write."
The Pen said to the Poet, "Use me!"
The Paper said to the Pen, "Just hold still."
The Poet said to the Paper, "Let him be."

The Paper said to the Poet, "Well write on."
The Pen said to the Poet, "What do you think?"
The Poet said to the Paper, "This is just too
hard."
The Pen said to the Poet, "Look there's the ink."

The Poet said to the Paper, "I think I'll retire."
The Pen and the Paper said, "Try harder."
The Poet said to the Paper, "Inspire me some!"
The Pen said to the Poet, "You're the master."

The Pen said to the Poet, "Look maybe it's best
we stop. You've asked the plainest thing around
to evoke both word and thought."
"Ahh but you see", the Poet said, "It's when
looking at Paper, words are stirred in my head."

"And besides", said the Paper, "I'm not plain,
I'm lined".
Then the Pen exclaimed, "I know I'm not blind!"

"That's enough you two", the Poet said, "I'm
trying to create here, I need quiet in my head."

The Pen said to the Poet. "I have the finest nib
around, a little ink and genius will abound."
The Paper said to the Poet, "I will do my utmost
Sir, to render images that provoke great
literature, that would pierce one's very soul".
"Right!" said the Poet, "All ready? Let's begin."

Encounter

It's **electric** and **raw** and **fresh** and completely **natural**.

It's **EYE-OPENING,**

breath-holding,

surreal, **awakening** and **POWERFUL.**

The Father of life touches me   and I'm off,

you won't stop me,
you won't see me,

I'm already gone.

Never to be the same again.

Mirror Talks (Girls)

Am I still pretty? Just checking
Do my eyes still pop? Just checking
Have I put on weight, lost weight? Just checking
Are my arms still strong? Just checking

Are my teeth nice and white? Just checking
Does this fit me right? Just checking
Has my hair grown long? Just checking
I'm sure nothing's wrong but I can't help still
checking

Am I still pretty? Just checking
Someone said I was beautiful. Is it true? Just
checking
How many times have I looked in the mirror
today?... One more. Just checking.

Mirror Talks (Boys)

Am I still on point? Just checking.
Need to get me some protein?
Just checking.
These shoes alright? To kick ball…? Maybe not,
just checking.
I need to re-tie these laces, just checking.
Should I comb my hair, wash my face?
Just checking
Are my teeth nice and white? Just checking.
(Tut) I'm due a shape up, just checking.
Do I need to press this shirt? Just checking.
Mum said " Press de shirt"…
Is this good enough? Just checking.
I like to wear my clothes a little tighter, you
know… This is alright, just checking.
Is this enough sag? Yhhh, just checking.
I'm looking nice, just checking.

Nahh, I need a shave, just checking.
Am I still on point? Just checking.
Is my skin ashy? Just checking.
Need to hit that gym haaarrrd!
Just checking.

Am I bulking or cutting?
Just checking.
Gotta see them abs, Just checking.
Is my hair out of place? Just checking.
Should I wear this belt 'round my waist?
Just checking.
Black Forces or J's?
Just
checking.

Mirror Talks (Boys and Girls)

What do I look like when I eat? Just checking
What do I look like when I speak? Just checking
What do I look like when I sleep? (Grimace)
Have I reached my mirror quota for the day?
Just checking. Wouldn't want anyone to think
I'm vain, or worse insecure.

Mirror Talks Back

Mirror talks, don't speak.
My my I can't believe
how these kids fail to see
the beauty that is within.

So don't mask it with make-up, don't distract
from it with tight clothes.
Edify and enhance it with wisdom,
understanding and knowledge, which comes
from God.

So don't ask me if you are still pretty, or if you
are still on point. Know the God of Heaven
Loves you and has made you Fearfully and
Wonderfully, with everything you need. Treat
your temple as you should and it will serve you
well in the days to come.

Do you know that when staring into a mirror
hardly anything changes or has changed. By
doing so you are looking for imperfections,
things out of place, doesn't that strike you as
wrong?

So next time you visit, please remember these
three things:
*You were made Fearfully and Wonderfully
*You are loved beyond your wildest dreams
And
*You can do anything you put your mind to,
with the help of Christ because He has already
given you what you need.

Pray Without Ceasing

Pray as you walk, Pray as you pray
Pray as you sleep
Pray as you wake
Pray as you dance
Pray as you sing
Pray as you talk
Pray when you're cooking

Pray as you eat, Pray as you pray
Pray as you watch
Pray as you play
Pray as you jump
Pray as you sit
Pray as you ought tc
Pray in the Spirit

Pray as you wash, Pray as you pray
Pray as you clean
Pray as you sway
Pray as you dream
Pray as you do
Pray with an honest heart
And God will honour you.

Real life installations

Real life installations, beautiful and prolific, challenging the status quo of the pavement and encroaching on our lives.
The inhabitants, heads bowed down, no visible eyes.
Are they lost in the midst of shame or do they shut it out, rejecting the rejection that has been their shroud?
They radiate heartache sometimes you know, or is it me as a passerby projecting?
Perfect and beautiful, real, they sit in different worlds made of paper, cardboards and thin sheets.
Who will deliver them, who will go ahead?
Me, what do I have to give?

Case study 58

I met myself as a case study
And for the purposes of anonymity
I'll call her number 58.
58 was lonely but not alone, saddened by her
low estate.
58 had a boyfriend, much older and a baby on
the way.
Such joy wrapped in such sadness, caused by her
low estate.
58 recounted to me the emotions that she felt.
She was sad because people sniffed the air and
said that she smelt.
At arm's length, she stayed from the world yet
they still moved her on.
Then one day their wish was granted, for she
had packed her things and gone.

Slightly naive childhood rant about death

No one is allowed to cry at my funeral
No one is allowed to wail at my grave
My passage should be filled with songs and
jubilance
For I'm going home, to my prepared place.
My Father in Heaven will receive me in Love
and I'll be immersed in the things of God
everyday.
So throw me a going away party, if you must
I'm simply emigrating to my prepared place.

I charge you to have a dewy eye or even dare to
sniffle
I know as humans we have a different affinity
for earthly life
but it pains me how much we allow grief to
cripple.

Death can be hard, unfair, unsympathetic,
Unmerciful and unexpected.
At times you feel alone and out of sorts.
Though is this just a mindset we've lent
ourselves to?
Should we be even sad at all?

I guess everyone deals with loss in different
ways and you are always going to miss someone
when they are gone.
Be encouraged that true life is a gift that has
been given and just goes on and on and on and
on.
And besides you'll have the memories and
photos to look over, till we meet again and we
will meet again!!!!!
As our earth suit expires, we need to relocate to
an atmosphere conducive for our new state.
Sooooo it may sound harsh but…

No one is allowed to cry at my funeral
No one is allowed to wail at my grave
My going away party should be fun.
Let the dead bury their dead, I'm merrily going
to my prepared place.

Haiku written at a more mature age

Grieving is healing
We need to get feelings out
Allow yourself time.

The Age of War

We are living in an age of war,
the consequence far past
We are living in a time of peril, of bombs,
machetes and masks
We are living in a class of war where the
military are top
We are living in an age of war
where time will pass, but no stop.
We are living in an attitude of war where
everyone makes their statement
We are living in a barricade of war,
where people are piled on the pavements
We are living in a barrage of war, where the
influx never stops
We are living in a legacy of war, where guns and
violence are polished and packaged for the local
shops.

This heirloom is deceptive and dangerous you
know, stripping humanity of its very soul.

We are living in a divide of war
where there are clear winners and clear losers
We are living in a mind-set of war,
where the velleity is to be more ruthless

We are living in an age of war,
when will this one pass?
When peace prevails and joy is rife,
we can all breathe easy at last.

Beautiful Sacrifice, the cost of Cherut

You bleed to get me out of the darkness
You bleed so I shed all my shame
You bleed so I have a chance to live the life You
intended and so I can stand proud in the
resurrection of my true identity and my new
name!

My darkness is gone by your stripes
My healing required by your stripes
Your protection I know, with faith there is so
much more (let the reader understand)
My past chains are gone by your stripes.

Selah

What a great weight you bore for me. Selah
So heavy with each painful breath on the cross.
How immense the pressure on Your lungs.
Your breath bursts forth and shares new
abundant life. Being near you makes me come
alive.

What a dear response that Your love saw fit, to
die for me and gathered words of wisdom;
revelation, life, light, knowledge and insight.
Understanding, overstanding, truth, blessing,
from within and showered on me; the former
and the latter rain. To watch me grow in
preparation for mission, destiny, good works,
greater things and the least of these.

Let this inspire true spiritual worship, that
affects movement in the heavenly realms,
bringing destruction to the plans of the enemy.
Let this inspire: great eruption and revelation of
Love. Let this inspire sustained fiery fervour.
Consider the sun, it takes pride in its worship.
Fulfilling its purpose, we feel its heat as it makes
its circuit from one end of the heavens to the
other. We may try to construct artificial realities
and play at changing the building blocks of life,
But God, the sun shines for You! May all people
recognise this and be moved to unabated action.

Tefillah

Dearest Father, closest friend
To the God that has continually exploded all my
barriers and boxes.
Tears down all my negative and corrupted
imaginations and replaces them all with Cherut
and Shalom.
I bless you, with all my heart.
Amen.